SHARING GOD'S BLESSING

HOW TO MINISTER TO PEOPLE

GRANT CRARY

SHARING GOD'S BLESSING
HOW TO MINISTER TO PEOPLE
by Grant Crary

Cover design by Kristen Ide

All scripture is taken from the New King James Version. Copyright © 1982 by Thomas Nelson, Inc. All rights reserved. Used by permission.

Printed in the United States of America.

Published by:

Fairdale Publishing

www.fairdalepublishing.com

Dedication

This book is dedicated to my wife, Jillian. She exemplifies the qualities that we need to minister effectively to people, in love, in wisdom, and in the gifts of the Holy Spirit. It has been such a joy to have seen the Lord work through her to bless others.

CONTENTS

INTRODUCTION

What do we mean by "ministering to people?" Simply put, we are referring to our being a means for the Holy Spirit to impact the lives of others through our counsel and prayers. Although God can, and does, touch and impact lives directly, it is more common for Him to work through people to bless other people. This might occur in a number of different ways, perhaps through the operation of one of the gifts of the Spirit such as a word of knowledge or a healing, perhaps through an answer to a prayer, or through wise advice.

In this book, we are discussing aspects of how we can minister to people and be someone through whom God can impart His blessing in whatever form that should take. A person might ask us to pray for them regarding a particular need or situation in their life, and to pray for them is an aspect of ministering. However, what we are mainly intending to cover in this book is the blessing of God speaking into the situation. For example, a person might request prayer regarding the need for a job, but as we talk with them, we sense something from the Lord, such as His teaching them to overcome fear in these kinds of situations. We can discuss this with the person and pray for God to help them in it. As a result, because we heard the voice of the Lord, what began as a prayer request for a job developed into a broader ministry to the person, one that may have positively impacted several areas of their life.

In this book, we will frequently use certain terms. Some of these are:

- **A word from the Lord.** By this we mean something that the Lord conveys to us to pass on to another person. We will refer to "having a word" for someone, which could come through a word of knowledge, a word of wisdom, a word of prophecy, or the some other gift of the Spirit. The Holy Spirit works through us in these gifts as the situation requires. The "word" may be a single word, but usually it is a sentence or more, or a passage from the Bible.

- **Ministering.** This refers to our being a channel for God to bless another person. "Ministering" may take the form of counselling, operating the gifts of the Spirit, encouraging, or any means by which God works through us to bless or help another.

- **The voice of the Lord.** Rarely will this be a voice that we hear, like when we converse with a friend. Nevertheless, it is the Lord "speaking" to us in some manner. He might place a thought or specific words into our mind. It might be a sense or an impression. It will not be something that we thought out for ourselves, but something that the Lord imparts to us.

It is a wonderful experience to know the Lord working through us to bless others. The person we are ministering to is blessed, but we are blessed too. For us, it may be the presence of the Lord as He comes to touch the person, or it could be the satisfaction of knowing that He made a difference in someone's life through us. Knowing His working through us to bless another person is truly a wonderful privilege.

This book has been prepared to provide an introduction to ministering to others. It is my prayer that it will encourage you, the reader, to seek the Lord to teach you and to equip you to be a blessing. If you are troubled that this is a giant step for you, please remember that everyone has to start somewhere. At some point, we have to make the decision that we are going to minister to others, and to ask the Lord to bless others through us. Find an avenue where you can regularly be praying for people. If you have a heart to be a minister and be a blessing, I am confident that He will work through you, "exceedingly abundantly above all that we ask or think" (Ephesians 3:20).

SHARING GOD'S BLESSING

HOW TO MINISTER TO PEOPLE

one

QUALIFICATIONS TO MINISTER TO OTHERS

What are the things that qualify us to be able to minister to others? Expressing this question in a different way, we could ask ourselves what God looks for in a person to make that person a capable vehicle to transmit His blessing. Here are some things that I have observed as being common factors in the lives of people who have become proficient in personal ministry.

(1) Having a heart to minister.

God did not make us all the same. We don't have to think very hard to know that each one of us is different from all the others. In many cases, the differences are very pronounced, and yet God causes us to be able to work together because of our common love for Him, and because we all have a unique contribution to make.

Our differences are obvious when we look at the occupations that we pursue. They vary greatly. Some like outdoor work, such as construction or farming. Some derive their satisfaction from directly helping others, such as in medicine or social work. Others prefer relative solitude and may be suited for research. Just as we have differing interests in our work, so too do we have differing interests regarding our place of serving in God's church. Some have a great passion for reaching those who don't know the Lord, some are fulfilled in administration, others in greeting. All of the aspects of serving are important because they combine to account for all of the many needs in the church.

Therefore, the first qualification to ministering to others is to have a heart for that aspect of serving. If it is not something that we desire to do, we will not do it well, and certainly we will not develop in our proficiency. Ministering to others can be inconvenient, and it can be time-consuming. It involves listening to the problems of other people, which is something that we have to learn how to handle so that their problems do not impact us as well. If we do not have a heart to bless others, we will never develop an ability to minister effectively to them.

I am reminded of a man who God used in some wonderful ways. Initially, he had no particular spiritual gifting that would enable him to serve in this manner. In fact, the lack of gifting was something that he readily admitted. However, he had a heart for people and could be counted on to make himself available to pray for others as the needs arose. He did not try to be someone that he was not, but contributed in small ways as he ministered alongside someone else. In time, God began to heal people through him, and steadily, certain other gifts of the Spirit became evident too. He then was able to minister effectively in his own right, and to lead others in ministry. It all began with just one qualification...having a heart to minister to others.

(2) A righteous life.

It is true that God can use anyone, and sometimes the most unlikely people operate spiritual gifts. This is because the ability to do so, at least at some level, does not require a deep spiritual walk. We can see this in the Bible, looking at the feasts of Israel, which have meaning in the spiritual life of a Christian. The Feast of Passover represents salvation, where the lamb was killed and its blood applied to the header and uprights of the doors of the Israelite's homes. When the angel saw the blood, he "passed over" those homes, and the lives of their firstborn children were spared. Similarly, when we receive Jesus and commit our lives to Him, the blood that he shed is a covering for us, our sins are forgiven and our relationship with God is restored.

The next major feast, the Feast of Pentecost, represents the baptism in the Holy Spirit with the accompanying gifts of the Spirit. Just as Jesus died at the time of the Feast of Passover for our salvation, the Holy Spirit was first outpoured on people at the time of the Feast of Pentecost (Acts 2:1-4). When we look into the requirements for these feasts in Leviticus chapter 23, we find that Passover was eaten with unleavened bread (verse 6) but at the Feast of Pentecost, the bread was baked with leaven (verse 17). Leaven, in the Bible, usually represents sin, hypocrisy, and false doctrine (but sometimes it is simply leaven).

Symbolically, the feasts declare to us that at salvation, all our sins are forgiven and we are cleansed from them by the blood of the Lamb. We are made righteous in the sight of the Father because of the blood of His Son. However, righteousness is also something that we progressively grow in. At our salvation, there are traits and actions that have to be dealt with as we mature in our Christian life, many of which are serious and many of which we do not recognize as being sin at that time. The inclusion of leaven at the Feast of Pentecost symbolically shows that attaining spiritual maturity is not a prerequisite to being baptized in the Spirit and operating spiritual gifts. Actually, the baptism in the Holy Spirit is given to help us get there.

The fact that the operation of spiritual gifts is not dependent upon our being mature Christians, or having attained to a high degree of righteousness in our lives, explains why we sometimes see problems in their operation. This was the case in the Corinthian church, prompting the apostle Paul to write at length on the correct operation of these gifts in a church meeting. The fact that there is sometimes improper functioning of these gifts does not mean that we should avoid them but rather that we should provide sound instruction regarding their correct use.

We might ask if the gifts of the Spirit can be given to immature Christians, who may operate them improperly or unwisely, why is righteousness a qualification for ministering with those gifts? The reason is that we need to grow in our level of competency. A person who lives a life of questionable righteousness will be limited in their ability to hear the voice of God, whereas those who walk closer with Him will hear more clearly. Psalm 25:14 says that "The secret of the Lord is with those who fear Him, and He will show them His covenant." In other words, if our lives demonstrate right-living in accordance with His commands, and a deep love and respect for Him, He will reveal to us things that will not be apparent to others. We may be able to operate gifts of the Spirit to some degree as immature Christians, but we will not develop in our effectiveness without living a righteous life. We must grow in the depth, power, and consistency of operation of these gifts, and living righteously before the Lord is an essential ingredient for this to happen.

(3) A good understanding of the Bible.

Without a good understanding of the Bible, our ability to minister effectively will be limited. It is not sufficient to know some Bible stories and have read the gospels. We need to understand the principles contained in this wonderful Book, brought out in both the Old and the New Testaments, so that we know how God views situations and how great men and women of God thought under the guidance of the Holy Spirit.

Without a good understanding, we will not be able to employ Bible principles in our ministry, which will severely restrict our effectiveness. Being able to apply the Bible correctly brings authority to a situation and is an essential aspect of ministry. In addition, it is common for the Lord to give a verse of the Bible for us to convey when we are ministering to someone. This is very helpful, as the person may forget much of what we say but they will remember the verse of Scripture. Therefore, a sound knowledge and understanding of the Bible, and its principles, is vital to an effective ministry.

7

How can we achieve a good understanding of the Bible? Well, most importantly, we must read it regularly. We can benefit from sermons and books, but we will learn the most from our own study. There simply is no substitute for regular, consistent reading of this amazing Book. It may seem a daunting task just to read it in its entirety, and often it seems that we can't even remember passages that we read only earlier in the day. However, the sense of what we read will remain with us, and the Holy Spirit will bring verses back to our recollection.

Hebrews 6:1-2 lists six doctrines that the writer describes as being foundational. It is important that we understand these doctrines. They cover the following aspects of the Christian life:

- Turning away from sin and things that hinder our walk.

- Having faith in God.

- Baptisms (in the plural, so this includes the baptism in the Holy Spirit; understanding the purpose and value of trials; becoming a Christian, part of the body of Christ; and water baptism by full immersion).

- The laying on of hands.

- The coming resurrection of the dead.

- The eternal judgement of all people that God will determine.

It is interesting to note what God considers to be foundational. No doubt, we would have included some of the above, such as faith in God, but would we have included the laying on of hands? If these six doctrines are considered to be foundational, we must understand them properly in order to progress in our faith.

Another passage from the Bible that speaks of spiritual growth is found in 2 Peter 1:5-11. The apostle Peter presents eight steps to maturity, and I believe that the Lord teaches them to us in ever increasing measure, rather than our learning one step fully before moving on to the next. We should note what Peter says about these truths. He says that if they are in our life, we will be fruitful in our knowledge of Jesus, but if they are not, we are shortsighted, blind, and have forgotten that Jesus cleansed us from our sins. He also says that if we do these things we will never stumble. Probably all of us can think of someone who had a significant ministry, but stumbled. Sometimes that stumble is very serious, so much so that the person never recovers, and others are seriously impacted. Therefore, we should pay attention to Peter's encouragement to us, and how we can be protected from having a disaster in our own lives.

(4) Common sense.

Common sense is an important ingredient to effective ministry and should not be overlooked. As my father-in-law likes to say, some people are so heavenly minded that they are no earthly good, meaning that a person can be so "spiritual" that they are not practical in their Christian walk. Maintaining a good, common sense approach, coupled with being alert to whatever the Holy Spirit might say, is how we should minister.

When we hear testimonies of God's leading, they always concern situations where the action taken was counter-intuitive. It is not very interesting to say that when I was out of work, I looked for a job through an employment agency, followed up on my contacts, and through my diligence a job opened up for me. It is much more exciting to have a story about finding a job because God brought someone from another country who prophesied that I should look in an obscure place that I never considered, and through some amazing series of events, I landed the job of my dreams.

I do not want to belittle the fact that God does indeed move in amazing ways, and I have certainly experienced this on many occasions. However, there is nothing unspiritual about taking a common sense approach to a ministry situation. When ministering to others we should not be hesitant to state the obvious. Sometimes people are looking for something supernatural, as if that would be the assurance that their guidance is from God, but common sense is the usual path. At the same time, when ministering we must be attuned to the voice of the Holy Spirit speaking to us, because sometimes He does direct in ways that are not obvious.

(5) Be baptized in the Holy Spirit

In the book of Acts, we find that the gifts of the Spirit began to function after the people were baptized in the Holy Spirit. One example is when Paul met a group of believers in Ephesus, as recorded in Acts 19:1-6. Paul sensed that these people were missing something and by asking the appropriate questions he found that they had not been baptized in a Christian water baptism, perhaps because they had not received the Lord, nor had they been baptized in the Holy Spirit. After some instruction, he baptized them in water and then prayed for them to be baptized in the Holy Spirit, upon which time they began to exercise spiritual gifts, in this case speaking in tongues and prophesying.

While it is true that God can do anything, and can even overrule Hos own principles that He has set in place for us to follow, it is also true that the gifts of the Spirit accompany the baptism in the Spirit. If we want to see these gifts functioning in our life, we must be baptized in the Spirit. Just as we read in the account of Paul and the Ephesian believers, the baptism in the Spirit is an experience for us to receive, subsequent to the experience of salvation.

t w o

TWO ESSENTIAL INGREDIENTS

I f we are to minister successfully, there are two qualities that must be incorporated into our ministry. They are love and wisdom. We will elaborate on each.

Love:

The apostle Paul wrote in so many words that, no matter how gifted he was, if he did not have love he was only making an ugly noise (1 Corinthians 13:1-3). That is very strong language that could be surprising to many people. Some of us value talent and ability above Godly qualities, but Paul stated the precise opposite. I have seen situations when the person ministering was absolutely correct in what they said, but the manner in which the word was conveyed did not impart life. A person might operate a spiritual gift but if the message is delivered in a condemning manner, it does not build up the other person. Frequently, it has the opposite effect, one of crushing the person's spirit.

How then would we describe ministering in love? Certainly, it is not some wishy-washy, watered down, politically correct method of delivering a word from the Lord. That was not how the prophets of old operated, nor how the New Testament apostles wrote their letters. Let us return to Paul's discourse on love to see how he described it. He said that love can put up with difficulties with a good attitude, it is kind, humble, polite, and not self-seeking. (1 Corinthians 13:4-7). This is the heart and spirit with which we must minister to others.

We must always be seeking the best for others, just as the Lord did in His ministry on Earth. A good example is His handling of the situation that occurred when a woman had been caught in the very act of having an adulterous relationship (John 8:2-11). Jesus must have sensed that she was truly repentant so He said to those present, who were her accusers, for the one who was without sin to cast the first stone for her execution. One by one, the accusers began to quietly slip away, their consciences pricked by Jesus' words. When all the accusers had left, there was no witness remaining to condemn her, and at least two witnesses were required by the Law. Jesus did not excuse her sin, even saying that she was not to do it again, but He set up the circumstances so that she could be restored. When we minister in love, we will bring the nature of God to the person, just as Jesus did to this woman.

I can recall a time when my wife and I were present while someone was ministering to another person. The word that the person gave, I do believe, was correct. However, the tone of voice and the choice of words used to convey it left the recipient devastated. I personally was quite shocked to hear it. The outcome was that the actual message was lost because of the manner in which it was delivered. Sometime later, God in his goodness gave the correct explanation to my wife who was able to inform the person and clarify the word that had been spoken, helping the person to be able to understand and embrace what God had actually said. Initially however, what was spoken had the opposite effect of what was intended. The person, instead of receiving insight into a situation that would help them walk through it, received a crushing blow.

How could this man have ministered differently? Sometimes the Lord will give us a thought but we need to consider how best to speak it so that it can be received. This is the essential nature of communication – the message must not only be spoken but it must also be correctly understood by the recipient, because otherwise, there has not been true communication. The man could have paused to consider how to phrase the word, asking the Lord to give him the right way to say it, and the right choice of words. He could have asked the Lord if there was something else as well, which may have clarified what he said. Had he just thought about the impact that his words would have, I am sure that he could have phrased it differently while still conveying the same message.

How we deliver the word is so important. I am reminded of a time when a man gave a word to another man, telling him that God had given him a gentle spirit so that he could deliver a difficult word, even when it is something that a person might not want to hear. Such a word will often be one of correction, and to deliver it in a harsh, judgmental tone may well result in the recipient rejecting it. The word must be delivered clearly, without ambiguity, but in love – kindly, humbly, positively, and if possible, with encouragement. This man had correctly understood that how a word is presented is just as important as the word itself.

God is so gracious. If we ask Him to help us show love in our ministry, He will do it.

Wisdom:

The other essential ingredient when ministering to others is wisdom. We saw a lack of wisdom in the incident recounted above, where the man could have paused to consider how best to phrase what he said before delivering it. It would have been wise to have done so. We must never lose sight of the fact that we are ministering to people, not objects, and people are precious to God. What we say and how we say it is so very important.

Let us consider another example. Suppose you are ministering to someone and you sense the Lord speaking the word, "murder" to you. What are you to do? You could say, "The Lord shows me that you are a murderer." If you do say something like that, you had better be right, because you have painted yourself into a corner. If the person denies it, you have nowhere to go. You declared that God has said it, and He knows everything, so it cannot be wrong. You will have lost the ability to minister to them, besides placing yourself in a very awkward position.

But perhaps you have the right word but the wrong application. A better way to introduce the word that the Lord has given to you would be to say, "I am sensing that God is saying something about murder. Does that mean anything to you?" Then you find that a close relative of this person was murdered some years ago. The heartache of that event had been bottled up and the memory had lingered and impacted the person to this very day. Now, because of your wiser approach, you have the opening to say how God loves this person, and that He revealed this terrible deed in order to demonstrate that He knows every detail of our lives. Instead of the ministry being shut down, you have the opening to help bring healing from the traumatic event.

In our example, the word that the Lord gave to you was "murder." If you jump to the conclusion that this means that the person is a murderer, you might be wrong, with disastrous consequences. Wisdom dictates that we approach the ministry with care, not saying something that leaves us with no avenue to proceed. Instead, it is wise to address the subject in a way that it can be received by the person, and as a result, we will be positioned to minister effectively.

The book of Proverbs declares the value of wisdom in many different places. It tells us that wisdom is the principal thing (Proverbs 4:7). It also says that nothing we can desire can be compared to wisdom (Proverbs 8:11). Furthermore, it tells us that the fear of the Lord is where wisdom begins. This is like great rivers which have seemingly insignificant beginnings, high in a mountain range, but become significant waterways on their way to the ocean. We must not overlook the value of having the fear of the Lord, which will similarly produce a river of goodness in our life and to those around us. We must have that very deep awe and respect for Him, so that we would never want to do anything to displease Him. We must be faithful servants in whom He can be pleased. We put obedience to Him above our personal interests, and have the one desire of our heart being to know Him better and better. In essence, this is the fear of the Lord.

Just as with love, if we need more wisdom (and who of us does not), we can ask God to give it to us.

three

HEARING THE VOICE OF THE LORD

We often talk about how the Lord has spoken to us concerning something. However, since seldom does He talk to us in the same manner as we converse with other people, what do we mean when we say that He has spoken? What is it like to hear His voice?

The most common way that the Lord speaks to us is through impressions in our mind. I am using the term, "impression" to describe how the Lord speaks, but the key factor is that it is usually a thought, word, or words that come to us. It is not something that we have reasoned or thought up on our own. I will use this term "impression" as an all-encompassing term to cover how the Lord speaks to us, but again, the key factor is that it comes to us and is not something that we reason ourselves.

We may be talking to someone or perhaps praying, and an impression comes to us. The impression could relate to almost anything. It could be a sense of something that He is going to do in the person's life, perhaps insight into a problem that they are experiencing, or perhaps an example from a passage of the Bible. Sometimes it will be a specific word, phrase, or sentence. Sometimes a thought.

When we talk about hearing the Lord's voice, we are not referring to an audible conversation but rather to the sense that accompanies the impression that comes to us. This is His presence, and what we come to recognize as His being the source of that impression. There is something unique about that sense, a peace and gentleness. Sometimes the impression is very strong, and sometimes so gentle that it can easily be pushed aside. Just as the Lord talked about sheep recognizing the voice of their shepherd (John 10:4), so too do we come to recognize His voice. We will do so more readily with time. The more we act on the occasions when He speaks to us, the more familiar His voice becomes. While the Lord might speak to us at any time, we will mainly just consider hearing His voice in situations when we are ministering to someone.

An example of His speaking to us could be a situation where we are counselling someone who wants to have a deeper walk with the Lord but they do not seem to be able to make much progress. We have an impression that at some time in the past, the Lord had told them that they needed to make peace with an estranged relative and they had not done so. The disobedience created the spiritual blockage that they are experiencing. This is the operation of the word of knowledge, where the Lord gives us information that we could not otherwise have known, so that we can minister effectively. The word of knowledge came to us in the form of an impression that the person had not acted upon this instruction from the Lord.

Another example might be an occasion when we are reading the Bible and a particular passage containing a certain promise almost leaps from the page, and we sense the Lord is saying that He is giving this promise to us. Or perhaps it is an actual word or words. I recall a time when I saw a young man several times over a period of a few weeks, and every time I saw him, into my mind came the words, "time management." I shared this with him, and sometime later I learned that these two words succinctly identified a problem in his life. The Lord wanted to help him, so He spoke to him through me, someone who did not know him well and had no idea that this was an issue.

There are many, many times in people's lives and ministry when the Lord spoke to someone through an impression. This impression can come while we are alone, while we are praying, or while we are with others. It could come directly to our mind, through a Bible passage, through a song, or almost any means. I remember once flying between two cities. I had a window seat and as I looked out, I could see houses, roads, and other evidences of civilization far below. It was a time when I was very burdened with cares in my life, but as I saw how small the objects on the ground seemed, I had the impression that my cares were also very small to Him, the One to whom I had committed my life, who knew every detail about me, and who was well able to meet my every need. It was an impression from the Lord of the relative greatness of God compared to my problems, and it was a wonderful encouragement to me.

Impressions in our mind are the most common way that the Lord speaks to us, and as we noted above, this could be a thought directly to our mind, or through some other vehicle such as the Bible. Other means could be through dreams, visions, through other people, specific sentences to our mind, and sometimes, though rarely, with words that we actually hear.

God, of course, is not limited. He can speak through any means that He chooses, as demonstrated when He enabled Balaam's donkey to speak to him (Numbers 22:28).

In ministry situations, we need to realize that the Lord speaks in different ways to different people. For example, there are people to whom the Lord will speak while they are simply sitting in a chair, giving them a word for the person or persons that they are with. As they look at a person in the room, a word from the Lord comes to them and they can deliver it to that person. They don't even have to get up to lay hands on the person, but the Lord gives them that word. My In-laws frequently minister in this manner.

Then there are others to whom the Lord speaks while they are conversing. As they are speaking to the person that they are ministering to, the Lord gives them a word that He wants conveyed. It comes out in the conversation, sometimes so naturally that it is possible that the hearer will miss the fact that it is from the Lord. Instead, they may view it as being really insightful advice. The Lord frequently speaks to my wife in this manner. She counsels many women, and I am often amazed when she tells me what the Lord gave her for a person. Sometimes it is a very simple thought, but sometimes it is something that I could never have imagined, and it usually comes to her as she converses.

When the Lord began to speak to me more consistently, it was almost always while I was actually in the act of praying for someone. I initially found this very difficult, because in my mind the way that the Lord would speak was quite different from that. My expectation was that He would give me a word for the person as I looked at them and "listened" for His voice, not necessarily remotely like the person sitting in their chair, but certainly before I began to pray. This was my preconceived notion of how He would speak, and it was based on having watched others minister in this manner. In addition, my preconceived notion included the expectation that the word He would give would be a thought that I would pass on to the person. Instead, I found that most of the time, I would receive a verse or passage from the Bible. In fact, the Lord still usually speaks to me with something from the Bible. It took me time to become comfortable with how the Lord would speak to me, but I became familiar with it by being willing to "go along with it." It used to be scary to approach someone to pray for them, knowing that I had absolutely nothing from the Lord, but in time I became confident that He would give me that verse or word if I was obedient and began to pray for the person.

When we first begin to hear the Lord speaking to us, we are usually unsure if it is Him. This is because we have not yet become familiar with His voice. We see this in the life of Samuel, who was a mighty prophet of God. However, when the Lord first began to speak to him as a boy, he thought it was Eli, the high priest calling out to him. Three times the Lord called to Samuel, and each time he arose from his bed and went to Eli to see what he wanted (1 Samuel 3:1-10). Later in his life, Samuel had become so familiar with the Lord's voice that he was able to receive and follow unusual directions, such as in the circumstances surrounding anointing Saul, and later David, to be kings of Israel.

So how do we begin to hear the Lord speaking to us? The way His "voice' sounds in a ministry situation is the same as when He speaks to us about other things. It resembles His nature...clear, peaceful, concise. Sometimes it is very pressing, like when someone is imparting an urgent message, but more often it is so gentle that it can easily be brushed aside.

What He says will not contradict the express words of the Bible. If someone should give us a word that essentially means we should steal something, it is a direct contradiction of a Bible principle, (in fact one of the Ten Commandments). Regardless of how we might respect the person, that word should be rejected. However, there are many situations when there is no directly corresponding passage in the Bible, but there are principles that we can follow. For example, there is a principle of our being generous, so a word given that contradicts this principle should be carefully prayed over before acting upon it.

The Christian life is one where faith is essential to our walk, and faith is involved in ministering to others. At some point, we have to take the risk that we might be wrong and deliver the word that we believe the Lord has given to us. We would love to see writings in the sky but it is highly unlikely that the Lord will do this. Rather, He wants us to be like the sheep in John chapter 10. The sheep have become familiar with the voice of their shepherd and when He calls, they follow. This is the same principle described in Hebrews 5:14 which says that mature Christians "have their senses exercised to discern both good and evil." We become more proficient at hearing God's voice as we grow in the Lord, and as we are obedient to, or "exercise", what He has given to us.

In life, everything has a beginning, and if we are to develop in our ability to hear the voice of the Lord, we have to actually start by presenting the word that we believe the Lord has given to us for another person, or by praying for them. That sounds very simple and logical, but some people just cannot bring themselves to start, even though they do want to minister to others.

It is the same with everything. If we want to ride a bike, at some point the trainer wheels have to be removed. If we want to drive a car, at some point we have to get behind the wheel. There is a certain a degree of risk that we have to take, because if we are wrong we will have embarrassed ourselves. But the Christian life is one of faith. The writer to the Hebrews stated that "without faith, it is impossible to please God..." (Hebrews 11:6), so we must exercise faith and take that risk. By operating with wisdom, we will shield ourselves from embarrassment, and most likely, we will find that we have indeed heard the voice of the Lord and that we have truly blessed someone.

Suppose someone asks for prayer. Perhaps they have a decision to make that is perplexing, and that is the focus of their mind. When we pray for them, we will certainly want to pray for their stated request, but as we pray, we must keep our spiritual ear open in case the Lord wants to say something. It may well be that the Lord will give us something else to pray for besides the request that was presented to us. We must not become so engaged in praying for the request that we miss that additional word that God would say through us. An important aspect of ministering to people is to be listening for the voice of the Lord.

It is important that we learn to hear the Lord's voice because we must minster by following principles, not rules. Once we have some experience in ministry, we might turn that experience into a rule, which may well prevent us from being led by the Holy Spirit in certain situations. I recall some years ago, that when someone received prayer for healing and they were not healed, the common reason that was given was lack of faith on the part of that person, or sin in their life. It is true that either of these conditions can be an obstacle to a healing, but to make that a rule is a serious mistake. Besides, it is very condemning. As we shall see in the chapter on the gifts of the Spirit, there can be a number of valid reasons why a person is not healed.

four

GIFTS OF THE HOLY SPIRIT

We are very fortunate that after Jesus ascended to heaven, He sent the Holy Spirit to be with us. One of the terms that Jesus used to describe Him is the Helper (John 14:16-17), and He most certainly is a helper to is when we are ministering to others. In truth, we would struggle without Him. While certain counselling disciplines and physiological training can be of assistance, there is no substitute for the operation of the gifts of the Holy Spirit. They enable us to pinpoint specific problems that could not be reasoned through our own analysis.

In 1 Corinthians 12:7-10, the Apostle Paul lists nine gifts of the Holy Spirit that are available to us. We will consider just five of them because they are the most common in personal ministry. They are the word of wisdom, word of knowledge, healings, prophecy, and discerning of spirits. The other gifts, faith, miracles, tongues, and interpretation of tongues have their place in ministry situations, but generally speaking, their use is in other situations.

The gifts of the Spirit are, as their name suggests, gifts that the Holy Spirit bestows upon us, and this He does according to His own will (1 Corinthians 12:11). These gifts operate through us on an as-needed basis. For example, we are not receiving words of knowledge all day, every day. That would be over-whelming for us, and unnecessary too. However, when we are ministering to someone, a word of knowledge might be very important in order to reveal some information that we could not have known, in order to conduct the ministry successfully.

The gifts of the Spirit are associated with the baptism in the Spirit, and while God can do anything, it is not common for these gifts to function consistently in the lives of people who have not been baptized in the Spirit. To operate the gifts of the Spirit, we need to have been baptized in the Spirit. Sometimes the operation of the gifts are referred to as "manifestations" of the Holy Spirit. This is a big word that means "showings," and it refers to those occasions when the Holy Spirit shows Himself through one or more of these gifts.

Sometimes it is difficult to determine precisely which gift was operating in a given situation. Was it a word of knowledge, or a word of wisdom? Perhaps, it was discerning of spirits, or perhaps, it was actually more than one gift that was operating. It really does not matter whether we correctly identify the gift because what is important is that the Holy Spirit worked through us to accomplish His purposes. However, we will attempt to provide a description of the nature of the gifts.

Word of Wisdom:

Through this gift, the Lord gives us a solution to a problem. It is not the same as wisdom that, in a sense, becomes resident in a person who is wise, Solomon being the obvious example from the Bible. Rather, it is the correct application of knowledge of a subject that we have to a specific situation, to solve a perplexing problem.

We can see this in the account of the Jerusalem Council in the Bible (Acts 15:1-29). The church leaders were faced with a dilemma, one that had the potential to divide the church. Gentiles had been coming to the Lord and the question was, did they need to follow the Law of Moses and in particular, the requirement of circumcision, in order to be saved. To a pious Jew of that day, it was unthinkable to fail to keep the Law, and circumcision was the sign of God's covenant with Abraham, so it is understandable that some Jewish Christians would hold this as being necessary, even for Christians.

After much discussion, the matter was solved when James, the head of the Jerusalem church, proposed that they require the Gentiles to keep only four provisions of the Law, which were largely common sense for a good Christian anyway, such as sexual morality and forsaking idolatry. They did not require the keeping of any rituals such as circumcision as being necessary for salvation. After what appears to have been lengthy discussion that had not produced an answer, in just a few minutes this contentious issue had been resolved. The Holy Spirit had given James a word of wisdom to settle the matter to the satisfaction of the differing parties.

On one occasion, I was asked to counsel someone who was experiencing many difficulties, and I really did not know what to say. I could not think of how to help the man, and platitudes would only be frustrating to him. As I silently prayed, asking the Lord for His insight, I suddenly realized the key to the main issue. It was something that he was neglecting. I had known others to have neglected this also, but it was not part of our conversation and not something that I would have reasoned to be applicable to this situation. Was this a word of wisdom or a word of knowledge? Possibly either, but I tend to regard it as a word of wisdom because it was based on knowledge that I already possessed, although I had not seen the application to this man's life. It proved to be the vital key to turning his situation around.

Word of Knowledge:

Through a word of knowledge, the Lord provides us with information that is pertinent to a situation that we could not possibly otherwise have known. It could relate to past, present, or future events, and it frequently provides the breakthrough in ministry situations.

An example in the Bible can be found in Acts 5:1-4. A man named Ananias and his wife, Sapphira owned a property that they decided to sell and give some of the proceeds to the church. This was a good and generous action on their part. They kept some of the proceeds for themselves, and gave some to the church. There was nothing wrong with retaining part of the proceeds for themselves, but they wanted the church to think that they had given the entire proceeds, so they lied about it. No one other than the couple could have known that they had secretly held back some of the money, but the Holy Spirit revealed to Peter what had really happened. This was a word of knowledge, given to Peter. He had no way of knowing the actual facts, but the Holy Spirit revealed them to him.

One time, my wife and I were counselling a young couple. They had known each other for some time and recently married, but for no apparent reason he began to exhibit outbursts of anger. This was not something that had happened before their marriage. The Lord showed my wife that in his past, there had been involvement with occult practices. As we talked about it, he realized that the involvement occurred when he was a boy, and actually only indirectly. His family would conduct séances, and although he did not participate, he would watch, and the spirit took advantage of a young, vulnerable boy. We prayed for him and broke this demonic hold over his life in the name of the Lord Jesus. Some months later, I happened to see the couple and was delighted to hear that he had not had any further outbursts. The operation of the word of knowledge enabled the breakthrough to free him.

We should note that often the operation of some of the gifts of the spirit is very powerful. For this reason, being able to minister in love is essential. We want to bring life to people, and to do so, we must have a love for them, even for those who have made terrible decisions and are suffering the consequences. Jesus died for them, just as He did for us, and who knows how well that person may finish if the Lord sets them free from their past.

Healings:

We should note that this gift is the gift of healings, in the plural. This acknowledges that there are many different healing needs, in our bodies, in our minds, and from the impact of past experiences. Sometimes the Lord heals instantaneously, sometimes over a period of time. We do well to keep this in mind because if a person is not healed immediately before our eyes, that does not mean that God has not heard our prayer. He will still be at work.

We also find that certain people will seem to see more healings of certain illnesses than others. I knew a man who had prayed for several people in the advanced stages of cancer and they had been healed. I knew another man who loved to pray for people with headaches because they were inevitably healed. I don't know why God would give this "specialization" but it is something that I have observed.

Sometimes, a person may need to be prayed for on more than one occasion before the healing takes effect. We see this in Mark 8:22-25, where Jesus prayed for a man's eyesight. Initially, his sight was partially restored, and he could see shapes that were not clearly defined. Jesus prayed again, and then the man could see clearly. Similarly, we sometimes need to pray multiple times for a person's healing.

Some illnesses are caused by evil spirits, as was the case with the epileptic boy in Matthew 17:14-18. Jesus cast out an evil spirit, and the boy was healed. We will recognize the work of the evil spirit by its behavior, and through the gift of discerning of spirits.

How then does the gift of healings operate? Sometimes, it is in conjunction with a word of knowledge. The Lord may show us that a person has a particular illness. This generates great faith in the person for their healing because they had not told us about the illness, so only God could have known the nature of the ailment. That said, I believe that faith needs to be present, but it can be the faith of the person who is praying, not necessarily the person with the illness.

I remember praying for a woman who had a rash that had started in her hand and was progressing up her arm. She had no idea what was the cause of the rash and was very troubled by the fact that it was advancing. I prayed, asking the Lord to heal her, and I had the impression that the rash would stop and reverse its course until her skin had returned to normal. I shared this with her, and when I saw the lady again a few weeks later and that was exactly what had happened. This was not an instantaneous healing but one that the Lord performed over a period of a few weeks.

Our basis for expecting the Lord to heal is rooted in His compassion for us. Many times in the Bible, we find that He was "moved with compassion" and healed people, even though He must have been very tired Himself. It is also rooted in the promise of Isaiah 53:5 which says that "by His stripes we are healed." I recall a man recounting a story about another man praying for someone to be healed. The man praying was speaking in tongues, and the language was Swedish, unknown to the man praying but recognized by the man who told this story. In a language he did not know, the man was praying, "You gave Your back for his healing," as the he cried out to the Lord to restore health to the man's body. The scourging and beating that the Lord took in His own body was for our benefit, His suffering for our health.

Although I believe it is the norm for us to expect the Lord to heal, there are occasions when this is not the case. In the Bible, we find that Paul had a "thorn in the flesh," which may well have been a physical ailment. (2 Corinthians 12:7). The Lord would not remove this for Paul's own good, so that he would not become prideful. We also find that Timothy had ongoing stomach problems (1 Timothy 5:23), and Paul had to leave a man named Erastus behind because the man was sick (2 Timothy 4:20). This is the same Paul who saw many amazing healings, so surely Paul would have prayed for the recovery of Erastus so that he could travel with him. There is also the case of the young son of King Jeroboam I who was ill. God said would die "because there was good in him" so that he would be spared the judgement that was coming on the house of Jeroboam (1 Kings 14:12-13). In His mercy, God took the boy. God looks with the eye of eternity, not just the temporal things that we tend to see.

It is clear that we do not have perfect understanding of healing. It is true that God heals, and we should pray for sick people, expecting God to touch their bodies and restore them to health. However, sometimes healings are not immediate, sometimes they are delayed, and sometime the person remains unhealed. All of this is in the wisdom of God. There was an occasion when my wife and I were asked to pray for a lady who had a particular illness. We did so, and that illness was not healed, at least not while we were present. We do not know if a healing took place later. However, the lady had another ailment that she had not mentioned, and the Lord chose to heal it immediately, even though we did not know about it or pray for it. As previously said, we do not have complete understanding of healing.

Prophecy:

The gift of prophecy is probably the most misunderstood of the gifts of the Spirit. This is because when we mention the word "prophecy," people tend to think of foretelling future events. There can be an element of this in the operation of the gift of prophecy, but the primary purpose is stated by the apostle Paul in 1 Corinthians 14:3 where he wrote that, "he who prophecies speaks edification and exhortation and comfort." Therefore, the gift of prophecy is a means for the Holy Spirit to speak words that will build up, encourage, and strengthen us. It may be a word for an individual, or for a larger group of people such as a church.

The gift of prophecy, one of the nine gifts of the Holy Spirit, needs to be distinguished from the ministry of a prophet, which we find mentioned in Ephesians 4:11-13. The ministry of a prophet is one of the five ministry gifts, given by Christ to His church to bring the church to maturity. A prophet is someone, appointed by the Lord, who brings the word of the Lord to His people. This may be edification, exhortation, and comfort, but it can also be correction, guidance, and foretelling. Prophets usually operate several of the gifts of the Spirit with extreme clarity. Let us summarize the differences between a prophet and the gift of prophecy, as they pertain to Christian people:

	A Prophet	Gift of Prophecy
Gift	A person, who is a prophet	Nine manifestations of the Spirit
Giver	Jesus	Holy Spirit
Recipient	The church	Usually individual Christians
Purpose	Bring the church to maturity	Building up individuals or a group of Christians

I recall a time when I was asked to pray for a young man. As I began to pray, I had a strong sense that God's hand was on him and His plan for this man's life was to accomplish some very significant things. Then, into my mind came a section from the parable of the sower where Jesus said that some seed fell amongst thorns which choked the word and it became unfruitful. Jesus identified the thorns as being, "the cares of this world and the deceitfulness of riches." I realized that although this man had the hand of God upon him, he could miss

God's plan because of concerns for other things, particularly material things. This was the operation of the gift of prophecy, encouraging him and also warning him. Interestingly, when I shared what the Lord had given to me, he agreed that he had a tendency to love things that would choke the word and prevent it from yielding fruit. Through the gift of prophecy, the Lord was warning Him to take care that he not be drawn aside and miss God's best.

It is appropriate to mention that when God gives a word in the form of a promise or insight into the future, it is not automatic that the word will come to pass. God's promise of love to us is unconditional, but prophetic words are usually conditional upon our walking in right relationship with Him, and being willing to step through a door that He opens. Just as Daniel prayed for the fulfillment of Jeremiah's prophecy of the Babylonian captivity lasting for seventy years, so too do we need to pray that the word that God has given to us will be fulfilled, and that we will perform any part that is required of us.

Discerning of spirits:

We sometimes hear people say that someone has the gift of discernment. Actually, there is no such thing in the Bible. The quality of being discerning may be likened to having wisdom, usually developed with time and experience. The gift that the Bible mentions is not discernment but discerning of spirits, which is more specific than being discerning. This gift enables us to recognize whether the Holy Spirit is present or some other spirit. It also enables us to identify what kind of evil spirit is at work, such as a spirit of witchcraft.

An example in the Bible occurs in Acts 16:16-18. A young girl followed Paul and Barnabas, declaring that "these men are servants of the Most High God, who proclaim to us the way of salvation." What she was saying was absolutely correct, and some might have thought that this must be God speaking to prepare the hearts of the people to receive the message from Paul and Barnabas. However, Paul, through the gift of discerning of spirits, realized that this was not God's doing and he cast the spirit put of her. Had the Holy Spirit not revealed this to him, it is very likely that the girl would have become the mouthpiece for the fledgling Christians of that city after the apostles left, leading the people away from the true faith in Christ.

I recall being in the presence of a man several times over a short period, and each time, there was something about him that agitated my own spirit. I don't know just how to describe it better; I just felt agitated within. It was nothing that he said or did, but when he spoke, something within in me was troubled. The man was very popular amongst many of my friends, but I became wary of him and avoided becoming too involved with him. This actually caused a breach in some friendships. However, a few months later, it was revealed that he was engaging in a practice that can only be described as a serious sin. Through the discerning of spirits, I had been alerted to that fact that something was wrong.

The gift of discerning of spirits operates through our senses, particularly hearing, seeing, and smelling. Perhaps a look in a person's eye reveals the presence of an evil spirit, or perhaps that spirit emits a foul odor. There will be something about the spirit that alerts us its presence.

five

KNOWING OUR ENEMY

Jesus said that He would build His church and the gates of hell would not prevail against it (Matthew 16:18). Gates do not attack anyone. Gates are constructed for defense. Their purpose is to enable the opening to the city to be closed off in order to protect the inhabitants from attackers. Therefore, Jesus was saying that the defenses of evil powers will not be sufficient to withstand the onslaught of the church. We have seen many instances where the spiritual weapons exercised by the church have defeated evil powers.

Let us now consider the characteristics of our enemies. While people may resist us and bring trouble upon us, the real enemies are the spiritual powers that influence them. It is an unavoidable fact that we will, from time-to-time, have to face situations where evil spirits are involved. They are very real beings and although usually unseen, they are evil, hate God, and seek to cause harm to people. They are more powerful than we are, but we have authority through Jesus to successfully stand against them.

Principally, our battles with spiritual powers are against demons. Demons are mentioned many times in the Bible, particularly in instances when Jesus cast them out of people. A number of different demons are specifically mentioned:

- Spirit of fear (2 Timothy 1:7)

- Spirit of infirmity (Luke 13:11)

- A dumb spirit (Luke 11:14)

- A lying spirit (1 Kings 22:22)

- An unclean spirit (Luke 4:23)

- Spirit of divination (Acts 16:16)

As to what other kinds of demons exist, we could say that there is one associated with most types of compulsive sin and also some illnesses. They are destructive, hate God, and seek only our harm. Demons themselves do not have bodies so they like to inhabit and oppress people or animals, and sometimes they may inhabit objects. I do not believe that a Christian can be "possessed" by a demon or demons, because possession speaks to ownership, and as Christians, we have committed ourselves to God, not to the devil. However, as we will discuss in the next chapter, a Christian can have an area of his or her life that is influenced by demons.

Demons can trouble people in various ways, and those under their influence inevitably cause problems for other people, such as in the commission of violent crimes. In some cases, they oppress a person by inhabiting their body, and in some cases by attacking from outside the body. A clear example of demons inhabiting someone occurs in the account of Jesus ministering to the man in the region of the Gadarenes who was inhabited by so many demons that they referred to themselves as "Legion" (Luke 8:26-40). From the description of his behavior, this man truly was possessed. When Jesus commanded them to leave the man, the demons realized that their time of possessing him was over and they begged Jesus not to send them to the Abyss but to allow them to enter a herd of pigs. The account shows that demons can inhabit both people and animals. It also shows that their ultimate destination is the Abyss which I believe is a reference to hell or to a section of hell.

An example of demons oppressing someone from outside their body, not inhabiting them, is found in 1 Samuel 16:14-23. Because of King Saul's disobedience, the Holy Spirit had left him. When a person habitually engages in some aspect of sin, they become vulnerable to being troubled by an evil spirit, and this was the case with Saul. However, when David would play his harp, the music would cause the spirit to leave Saul and he would feel refreshed. This was a situation where a spirit would oppress Saul from time-to-time, but it could be driven away by music. Worship music is, in fact, a very powerful weapon, and often the atmosphere of a room can be changed by playing good, Christian worship music.

UNDERSTANDING SPIRITUAL AUTHORITY

The authority of the Lord Jesus is the key to victory for us. Having discussed how these spirits are evil and powerful, we may wonder how we can successfully combat them. The answer is that we are not able to do so in our human strength, but fortunately, our victories are not dependent upon that strength but upon the strength of Jesus who defeated them on the cross. Here are some references that declare His supremacy:

- **Matthew 28:18-19** – "All authority has been given to Me in heaven and on Earth. Go therefore…"

- **Colossians 2:15 – Speaking of Christ's victory on the cross,** "Having disarmed principalities and powers, He made a public spectacle of them, triumphing over them in it."

- **Philippians 2:9-11,** "Therefore, God also has highly exalted Him and given Him a name that is above every other name, that at the name of Jesus every knee should bow, of those in heaven, of those on earth, and of those under the earth, and that every tongue should confess that Jesus Christ is Lord to the glory of God the Father."

- **Hebrews 2:8,** "…For in that He (the Father) put all things in subjection under Him (Jesus), He left nothing that is not put under Him."

Our success in spiritual battles depends not upon our strength but upon the victory of Jesus and the authority that He has given to us to act on His behalf. We see this principle in the story of the Roman centurion who had a servant who was desperately sick (Matthew 13:5:13). When the centurion told Jesus about his sick servant, He said that He would come and heal him. The centurion replied that it was not necessary for Jesus to have to come to his house but if He would just speak the word, the servant would be healed.

The centurion went on to explain why he knew this to be true. It was because Jesus was "under authority," in His case under the authority of the Father. The centurion related how he could instruct his servants and they would obey him because, "I also am a man under authority," in his case ultimately the authority of Caesar. The centurion understood that the key to his being able to direct his servants and their being obedient to him was because he himself was under the authority of those above him. He recognized that the key to Jesus' being able to perform miracles was His obedience to the Father. By living a

44

life of obedience, under authority, Jesus had the authority to act on the Father's behalf. To the centurion, it was no surprise that Jesus could perform miracles. He understood from his own experience, that being under authority, Jesus had the authority to do what He did.

Stating this a little differently, the centurion recognized that his commands to his servants carried the weight of the highest power on Earth, the Roman Empire and its Emperor. And he understood that Jesus' commands carried the weight of the highest power of the universe, God the Father. The centurion said that in one respect, he and Jesus were alike...they both exercised authority over those under them, and could successfully do so because they themselves were obedient to the authority that was over them.

The same principle is true for us. We do not possess the strength to defeat evil powers but it is not strength that we need. What we need is obedience to the Lord, or being under His authority. Then we can exercise that authority, and by our word, enforce the victory of Jesus over them.

In the natural state of affairs on Earth, the strongest power usually wins. This was particularly so in Jesus' day, when hand-to-hand combat was how wars were fought. The more soldiers in an army, the greater was the likelihood of victory. (Interestingly though, Israel is almost always outnumbered when they go to war, but God fights for them and history has recorded many astonishing victories for Israel). Consequently, when we come up against an evil spirit we have a tendency to try to exert power. For example, we may yell at the spirit to leave the person. However, the true power comes from Jesus. Our role is to exercise authority. The authority is the force that brings victory. It is not any kind of natural force that we could try to exert.

We can also look at this matter of authority from a slightly different perspective. When God created Adam, He said, "Let him have dominion over the...fish, birds, and every living thing." (Genesis 1:26). "Dominion" means to have "the power or right of governing and controlling, sovereign authority." This is seen in Genesis 37:8 when, after Joseph had told his dreams to his brothers, the brothers questioned his right to have dominion (or authority) over them, as was implied in the dreams. (The reason was that Joseph was the eleventh son, and in that culture, it was the eldest who would normally be given a position of superiority over his brothers). After Adam sinned against God, he lost that dominion. It passed to the devil, which we can see when he tempted Jesus in the wilderness. The devil promised Jesus "all the kingdoms of the world and their glory" if He would fall down and worship him. Jesus did not dispute the devil's right or his ability to make good on his promise, although knowing that he is a liar, one has to wonder if he would have done so had Jesus complied.

However, having gone to the cross and become the perfect sacrifice for sins, all authority has been given to Jesus in Heaven and on Earth (Matthew 28:18-19). There are no exceptions in this passage. Moreover, Daniel prophetically wrote of Jesus that "...His dominion is an everlasting dominion that shall not be taken away" (Daniel 7:14), and Peter wrote, "to Him be glory and dominion forever and ever" (1 Peter 5:11). So we see that Adam was given dominion over all the works of God on the Earth, surrendered it to the devil, but Jesus, the second Adam, took it back and will never lose it. His is the name above all others. Of course, we must be clear that in the period after Adam and before Christ, God had never surrendered His sovereignty. He has always maintained control. He may allow

46

certain things to happen, but it is always "until" the timing that He has chosen to put an end to those things, such we see as in Daniel 7:21-22.

We should realize that the devil's chief weapons against us are deception and fear. It is not at all uncommon to feel fear when confronting evil spirits, and I have been attacked in this manner many times when coming against demons in ministry situations. However, because I know the authority of Jesus, I can press past the attack. If we understand the victory of Jesus, we are secure in Him and fear does not have to hinder us.

The Armor of God

In Ephesians 6:10-18, the apostle Paul teaches on the armor of God. Just as a soldier does not go into battle without armor, so also we need armor for our spiritual battles. Paul used the analogy of the armor of a Roman soldier to illustrate our spiritual armor. The armor of God is discussed most ably in many other publications so we will provide only a brief overview here. The items that Paul listed are:

- **The belt of truth.** A belt holds everything together, and so having truth in our lives is essential. This truth is being truthful in our conduct. We must not be deceitful people. It is also having a sound knowledge and understanding of the Bible, the Word of Truth.

- **The breastplate of righteousness.** A breastplate is designed to protect our vital organs, such as our heart. Therefore, if we do not walk righteously, we can be vulnerable at the core of our life.

- **Shoes that are the preparation of the gospel of peace.** Shoes cover our feet, enabling us to walk over rough ground that would otherwise be painful to us. The spiritual protection for our walk in God is our motivation to bring the gospel of peace with God to others.

- **The shield of faith.** Everything in the Christian life involves faith. We must develop a deep trust in God, trust in the goodness of His nature and in His love for us. We must come to the place where we truly believe in our hearts that "all things work together for good to those who love God, to those who are called according to His purpose" (Romans 8:28). Many things happen in life that are hard to understand, sometimes very bad things, but we must know the nature of God sufficiently well that these things are not stumbling blocks to our walk.

- **The helmet of salvation.** Most of our battles take place in our mind, so the helmet of salvation is a vital piece of equipment. We are transformed by the renewing of our minds (Romans 12:2), so it is important to protect it. Understanding what Jesus has done for us, that our sins have been forgiven and fellowship with God restored, and having a future expectation of heaven, helps keep us in times when the devil attacks our mind.

- **The sword of the Spirit.** Paul tells us that this sword is the Word of God, the Bible. Understanding spiritual principles and living in accordance with them is essential. We would do well to remember that when Jesus was being tempted by the devil, He parried each temptation with a quotation from Scripture. On one occasion, the devil tried to outwit Him by quoting Scripture too, but his quote was out of context and Jesus, fully understanding Scripture, countered with an appropriate quotation. Each time, after Jesus quoted Scripture, the devil did not continue with that conversation because he knew that Jesus' understanding of Biblical principles meant the end of the matter.

- **Praying in the Spirit.** There is no question that prayer changes things. We can look at prayer as our secret weapon, one that enables us to go behind the enemy's lines and disrupt his camp. We may not be able to combat him directly but through prayer, we can change the circumstances.

Let us consider some questions relating to deliverance from evil spirits. Firstly, what do we mean by deliverance? The term refers to situations where we come against some work of an evil spirit in a person's life. This could involve dealing with a spirit that is within the person, oppressing them from outside, or a breaking of a spiritual hold over their lives. It is a situation where we exercise the authority of Jesus over these wicked beings to see a person freed from their hold over that person. While evil spirits and the nature of their attack upon us may have their differences, they are dealt with essentially in the same way. It is a matter of authority. Jesus defeated the powers of darkness, and His is the name that is above every other name. As His servants, walking in the light that He has given us, we order the spirit to leave and/or break the bondage in the authority of His name. We have authority because we are under authority.

Here are some frequently asked questions regarding deliverance:

Should we command the spirit to name itself?

This approach has its basis in Jesus' ministry to the man in the Gadarenes. This man was terribly possessed by evil spirits, to the point where his behavior was bizarre, and he had the strength to break chains. In Luke 8:30, Jesus asked, "What is your name?" A spirit, probably the chief of those within the man, answered and said, "Legion," because there were so many spirits in the man that they could be numbered like a military legion. Some people have taken this passage to show that we should command evil spirits to name themselves, and if we know their name we will then have control over them.

There are some problems with this perspective. Firstly, the spirit did not actually name itself when answering Jesus but essentially stated that there were many spirits in the man. Jesus did not then proceed to cast out a "spirit of legion," and nowhere in the Bible do we find Jesus or the apostles casting out a spirit that they commanded to name itself. The spirits that the Bible speaks of, such as a spirit of divination, were identified by the behavior that they exhibited. This is the operation of discerning of spirits, one of the nine gifts of the Holy Spirit.

Secondly, why would we expect that the evil spirit will tell us the truth? In particular, if we are dealing with a lying spirit or a deceiving spirit, we should actually expect that spirit to call itself by any name other than its true identity. Jesus said that the devil has no truth in him (John 8:44) and we should not expect evil spirits to be honest with us. Therefore, it is best to rely on the gifts of the spirit, particularly in this case the discerning of spirits, rather than expecting that a spirit naming itself will result in a successful deliverance.

As a young man, I had heard that we should command the spirit to name itself, and when I was asked to minister deliverance to someone, I commanded the spirit to tell me its name. The spirit called out several names which I tried to cast out, and in retrospect, I believe he was lying every time. The person was not delivered.

Sometimes demons will speak through the person that they inhabit and it is wise not to engage in conversation with them. We cannot trust anything that they say. Also, they are intelligent, and if we are not careful, we may unwittingly be lured into a position which is to their advantage. By engaging in conversation, we are allowing them an element of control over the deliverance, which will most likely be unproductive.

Can a Christian have a demon?

There are some who believe that a Christian can be troubled and attacked by a spirit that is outside his or her body, but that a Christian cannot have an evil spirit within their own body. The supposition is based on the thought that because a Christian has the Holy Spirit dwelling within, we would not expect an evil spirit to be there too.

However, the difficulty with believing that a Christian cannot have an evil spirit within is that there are many Christians who can testify to having experienced victory in an area of their lives following an evil spirit leaving their body. Sometimes the person is very aware of that spirit leaving them, and others who have been present have observed the evidence. This has been my own observation on no few occasions, when the person was undeniably a true Christian, and an evil spirit undeniably manifested itself within that person before being expelled.

An event that left a lasting impression on me as a young man was being with another man as he ministered deliverance to a young lady who I knew had been a righteous, committed Christian for many years. The Lord enabled him to see into the spirit realm and he saw the spirit within her. It is interesting to recount how he proceeded. He actually did not say a single word, but simply motioned with his finger to the spirit to leave. The room was quite small and crowded, but I doubt that anyone had the slightest idea that this man was ministering deliverance. It was a great lesson to me regarding authority. This man knew his authority in Jesus. He did not have to yell or in any way attempt to exert power. He didn't even speak to the spirit. However, because he understood his authority he only had to motion with his finger.

So the question then is, how can it be that a Christian can have an evil spirit within? I can give you my opinion, which is that at some point, usually prior to becoming a Christian but not necessarily, the person engaged in an habitual sin that opened the door to a spirit entering them, and that spirit still exercises control over that aspect of the person's life because it had been given over to them. Another means is when a spirit takes advantage of a vulnerable person, perhaps a young person or even a child, who was exposed to some situation that gave the spirit entrance. It could be a spirit of fear, taking advantage of a child who is terrified by a violent home situation.

A Christian having a demon within is like having a house with rooms that are clean and tidy but the garage is a mess. Most of the dwelling looks perfect, but there is this area that needs cleaning up and is not under control. For example, if a man engaged in occult practices, he may find that he just cannot seem to progress in his Christian walk. He may need deliverance from, for example, a spirit of witchcraft in order to break free from its hold.

Sometimes a person may have what I will call a spiritual bondage. This is slightly different from a demon inhabiting or oppressing the person. Instead it is, as the word suggest, an area of their life that has a tendency to some sort of destructive behavior and the person is bound to it. Frequently, these bondages come through the family. Just as we have physical characteristics that resemble our parents and grandparents, so too we might have a spiritual problem that we inherited from them. For example, if someone has a temper that they have difficulty controlling, we will usually find that their father, and perhaps grandfather too, had the same issue.

These hereditary bondages are real and can hinder our spiritual progress. On one side of my family, alcohol was a significant problem, and a number of my relatives shortened their lives due to alcoholic consumption. As a young

Christian, I was prayed over to have the hereditary bondage broken, and alcohol has never been an issue in my life, or in that of my children. However, the same is not true for my some of my cousins, who have had alcohol problems in their lives and in their children's lives too. I don't believe that I needed a deliverance, but I did need to have a spiritual bondage broken that could have resulted in a tendency to excessive drinking and severely impacted my life. A problem that had been passed through several generations was completely stopped with me.

If we receive a deliverance, are our problems in that particular area of our lives over?

Usually, a person experiences a considerable change following a deliverance from an evil spirit. This is precisely what we would expect. However, there is an important principle that pertains to deliverance found in Deuteronomy 7:22. Here the Lord said that He would not drive out the nations of the Promised Land all at once because if He did, the Israelites would not be able to hold on to their territory, so He would drive them out, little by little. It is not that a spirit is expelled from us little by little, but rather that having had that spirit expelled, we still have to reclaim the territory that is ours.

Suppose a person had a spirit of fear and received ministry to break that bondage and the spirit was expelled. The person may still have a period of time where he or she has to battle fear. The difference between before and after the deliverance is that the person will be able to win battles that could not be won before. Over time, the person gains the ascendancy and the attacks become less frequent and are conquered more quickly.

In His kindness to us, the Lord has us go through this period of battles to help us become strong.

Sometimes, too, the principle of Romans 12:2 is applicable in deliverance situations. This verse talks about our being "transformed by the renewing of our minds," and our way of thinking has to be changed by the Holy Spirit. We may have received our deliverance, but our thinking may need to be changed in order for that deliverance to be fully worked out in our lives.

If a person has a powerful ministry, is that evidence that they have a right relationship with God?

The answer is, yes and no. It is true that as we are more and more purified, our relationship with God grows, and frequently, so too does the power of the Holy Spirit working through us. However, we are told not to blindly accept everything we see and hear, but to evaluate. We are exhorted to "test all things; hold fast what is good" (1 Thessalonians 5:21). This is because God does not retract the gifts that He gives (Romans 11:29), so a person could continue to operate spiritual gifts in a powerful manner, even if sin has entered their life and/or their doctrines are polluted.

The Lord made clear that the Bible is the yardstick by which we measure. In Deuteronomy 13:1-5, we read that if there is a prophet who gives prophecies that do in fact come to pass, but he instructed the people to follow other gods, we should not listen to his teaching. The fact that the prophecies came about does not mean that the person's teaching is also correct, even if he is a prophet. As we measure the prophet's teaching by the Bible, we can see that it is contrary to the commandments of

God. The passage adds that God is testing us, to know whether we love Him with all our heart and soul. We are thrilled to see the demonstration of the power of God, and rightly so, but if it is accompanied by teaching that is contrary to the Bible we should not receive that teaching and follow it. Instead, we should be wary of the person's ministry. The test of conformity to the Bible can apply to the spirit of the person who is ministering as well as to his/her doctrines. For instance, if that person has an arrogance about them, we should be careful because arrogance is not a Godly trait. What they say may or may not be correct. We must test it by the yardstick of the Bible and not be enamored by the works themselves.

Why do some people not receive a deliverance?

There can be many reasons why a person does not receive a deliverance from a demon. We will look at two of the common reasons.

(1) Unforgiveness. Unforgiveness is something that can block spiritual growth in practically any area of our lives. After counselling many people over many years, I have found that it is the number one reason why people struggle to progress in their Christian walk. This is true for deliverance also. I have experienced situations where a person was not able to be freed from an evil spirit because they held a grudge against another person. God considers our attitudes toward others as a serious matter. He has completely forgiven us of all of our many sins, and it is important that we in turn, forgive others who offend and harm us. Holding onto that bitterness will often hinder our being freed from the influence of an evil spirit.

(2) Not wanting to let go of sin. Incredible as it might seem, there are some people who want to be delivered, but at the same time they don't want to turn away from a sinful behavior. We can't have it both ways, and our love for the sin will prevent us from coming free. Perhaps in some ways, it is a good thing, because Jesus said that if a spirit leaves a man and cannot find a new home, it will return with seven others and if it finds the old house vacant, it will re-enter and the person's end will be worse (Matthew 12:43-45). This shows that it is important for us to walk uprightly before the Lord and ask Him to fill us with His Spirit. Then our house will not be vacant, vulnerable to demonic attack and bondage.

Unfortunately, there are times when neither of these two explanations seem to answer the question as to why a person is not delivered. What should we do? Here are some suggestions:

- **Take a few days to seek the Lord for an explanation.** He may reveal something to us, or to the person who is seeking the deliverance.

- **Fast.** Jesus linking fasting to deliverance, and fasting may be what is needed to add power to the ministry.

- **Seek the help of another Christian who has experience with deliverance.** It is okay for us to be humble and acknowledge that we don't have all of the answers, all of the time. We are the body of Christ, and as such another Christian may be able to contribute to the ministry.

- **Question the person regarding occult involvement.** There may be some specific sin related to occult involvement that needs to be confessed.

- **Be open to the Lord providing further insight regarding the two points of unforgiveness and holding onto sin.** He may reveal something that the person has overlooked, or perhaps not wanted to talk about. Don't approach this in an accusatory manner, but be open to the Lord leading you.

CASE STUDIES

We will look at some ministry situations so that you can think about how you would handle them. Some of these situations could be addressed in more than one way, based on the facts that are presented to you, so your assessment may not match how the case was actually conducted, even if yours is a perfectly valid assessment. Also, you do not have the benefit of the Lord guiding you, as was the case when these events occurred. Nevertheless, I trust that they will stimulate your thinking as to how you might have handled them.

Some of the cases involve ministering to a person of the opposite gender, and although not mentioned in the write-up, whenever this happened the person ministering had another person present of the same gender as the person to whom they were ministering. This is the case with all illustrations in this book. It is not wise to minister alone to someone of the opposite gender.

Case 1: The situation

A woman comes for prayer for healing for a bad back. She injured it, had surgery, and it has been considerably worse following the surgery. She tells you how she has been a strong Christian woman who has attended church faithfully for many years. She talks about how she has served the Lord, and seems to be a good person. Everything she says sounds right. But as you listen, you sense that there is something that is not right, although you don't know what it is.

(a) What would you do? Would you proceed to pray for her healing?

(b) Would you ask her questions, and if so what kind of questions?

(c) If you determine that there is a problem of unforgiveness, what counsel would you give?

Case 1: What happened

My wife, Jillian, was conducting the ministry, and she sensed that, although everything the lady said seemed right, there was something else that was not obvious but nevertheless, pertinent to the case. This could be the gift of discerning of spirits, where we identify what spirit is operating, or a word of knowledge, where the Lord gives us information that we could not otherwise know. The lady had a slight edge to her voice when talking about the surgery so Jillian asked if she was angry over the surgery. The lady replied that she was angry at the doctors who had performed the surgery unsuccessfully, so Jillian asked if she had forgiven them. She had not, but agreed that she could confess her unforgiveness to the Lord and forgive the doctors.

However, Jillian still sensed that there was more to this so she asked if there was anyone else that the lady needed to forgive. The lady replied that she was angry at her children because they had not helped her or supported her. Again, after some discussion, she was willing to forgive them. But then she said, "I will never forgive my husband. I would rather keep my back pain than forgive him." And that is where it finished. The lady left, still with her back pain. Through the gifts of the Spirit, the Lord had lovingly brought to light the woman's greater need to forgive, but she chose to hold on to her bitterness.

In the Lord's Prayer, Jesus said to ask God to forgive our sins as we forgive others, so if we want to receive His forgiveness, we must be willing to do the same. The bitterness had to be dealt with in order for the healing to take place. As she walked away, the Lord spoke to Jillian saying, "She has made her decision", presumably a reference to the lady's preferring her pain to forgiving her husband. It is my belief that the situation could not be reversed without her being sincerely repentant.

Case 2: The situation

A woman comes for prayer and as she describes her situation, she becomes very agitated. Her voice rises and she begins to speak rapidly, waiving her arms as she recounts the things that are so troubling to her. The situation that she describes involves a moderate level of verbally abusive treatment (not that even a moderate level is acceptable), and although it would have been unpleasant, the lady's reaction seems excessive.

  (a) Do you consider her to be overly emotional? Is the appropriate ministry to calm her down?

  (b) How would you pray for her?

Case 2: What happened

As the lady was speaking, I sensed the Lord saying that she was being troubled by a tormenting spirit. This was the functioning of discerning of spirits. I allowed her to talk for only a short additional time because she was repeating the same things over and over. So, I interrupted her and explained that I would like to pray against an attack of the enemy against her. I came against the tormenting spirit in the name of the Lord Jesus and ordered it to leave her. Immediately, she calmed down, and within just a few minutes she was completely calm. I then gave her some instruction so she could rebuke another attack herself should one come.

Case 3: The situation

A lady comes for prayer for her marriage because it is in trouble. Her occupation is one in which she has to be insensitive to the people she deals with, and no doubt she has taken some of these "skills" home and they are affecting her marriage. She is blunt in her conversation, and anything you suggest, she says she has tried and it didn't work. In fact, she knows all the answers (at least in her own mind). After talking for about a half hour, you feel that you have made absolutely no progress and you don't see any reason to continue the conversation.

(a) What do you do?

Case 3: What happened
The lesson that you should take from this case study is never to underestimate the power of prayer. I felt like I had achieved nothing in this conversation and it was time to wrap it up by closing in prayer. I began to pray, and as I did, the Lord directed me to ask that certain fruits of the Spirit - patience, gentleness, kindness - be worked into her life. I finished, and expected that she would leave. To my surprise, she sat still in her chair, not saying anything. I realized that the Lord was at work so I also sat quietly, not understanding what was happening but not wanting to get in the way. After a few minutes, she said, "It's not optional, is it."

I still didn't know what was happening, and I didn't know what she was referring to, but knowing that the Lord was doing something I agreed with her. "No, it's not optional," I said. After a few more minutes of quiet, the lady said that she realized that she had to have the fruit of the Spirit in her life. Now I was beginning to understand what had happened. The Lord guided me to pray about the fruit of the Spirit, and as I did, He convicted her of her lack, and probably showed her how that lack was impacting her marriage. Instead of her leaving, our meeting continued for another twenty minutes, and this time she listened intently to everything I said.

A few weeks later, I saw the lady again. Very excitedly, she told me how she had changed her attitude toward her husband

and the marriage had transformed. Their love for each other was renewed and they were both very happy. In a very real sense, a moment of a prayer under the leading of the Holy Spirit changed everything.

Case 4: The situation

A man describes how, when he is in a meeting, the Lord causes him to feel in his body the needs of others. Sometimes it is ailments that need healing, sometimes it is sin. The weight of these experiences is often very severe and emotionally hard on him, to a point where he sometimes cannot attend church. He seems to be a sincere Christian with a good knowledge of the Bible.

(a) What gifts of the Spirit do you need to effectively minister to him?

(b) What questions would you ask to help determine how to minister?

Case 4: What happened

As I talked to the man, I believed that he was a sincere Christian, and that he was convinced that the experiences that he was having were a ministry that God had given to him to help others. I know of instances where people have felt illnesses and the like that pertain to others in their own bodies, but the degree to which this burden overwhelmed the man led me to suspect that this was not the Holy Spirit but an evil spirit at work.

To answer the questions posed in the case study:

(a) What gifts of the Spirit do you need? Discerning of spirits, perhaps also the word of knowledge and the word of wisdom.

(b) What questions would you ask? We would want to understand what has happened in the man's past that would leave him so vulnerable to such strong attack by the devil. So, I asked him if he had prior involvement with the occult.

As we talked, the man told me that he used to be in a cult and had had considerable involvement with occult things. He said that he had been prayed for to be delivered from the spirits associated with his past, and that he had been delivered. He believed that these current experiences were a ministry that God had given to him.

It was my opinion that he may have been prayed over for deliverance but there was still an evil spirit at work, causing him to have these experiences. I actually was not able to pray for him because he declined to meet with me. Had we met, I would have used the Bible to explain the nature of God, to try to help him realize that God doesn't treat us the way he was being treated by this spirit. If I was able to do so, I would then have asked him to renounce the contact with the evil spirit. I would have ordered the spirit to leave him in the authority of the name of the Jesus. I like to quote some passages from the Bible when praying for someone in these instances, such as Jesus being the risen Son of God, how He has all authority, and that every knee has to submit to that Name.

Case 5: The situation

A couple comes to you for prayer at the end of the service. The man says that his wife needs prayer because she is having a difficult time, and looking at her, you can see that she does indeed appear distressed. There is no time available to attempt to counsel the lady, or even to ask more that some cursory questions about the situation. There is only time to pray.

(a) How would you pray?

Case 5: What happened

In this situation, there was no time to ask questions, only time to pray. When praying for people, we always want to be "listening" to the prompting of the Holy Spirit. I began to pray for the lady, asking the Lord to comfort her and help her through this trying time. While praying, a passage from the Bible came into my mind and I incorporated it into my prayer. When I finished, the man spoke with quite an outburst of deep remorse, and when I looked at him, he had tears streaming down his face. He said that the previous night he had told his wife that he wanted a divorce, but when I mentioned the words of that Bible passage, he suddenly saw how hurtful his actions over the past had been. With great emotion, he looked at his wife, saying how sorry he was. They left to rebuild their marriage, and I went home wondering how the Bible passage could have brought about such a dramatic result.

The lesson from this case study is the need to be "listening" for the voice of the Lord. I could never have imagined the amazing result of presenting the Bible passage that He gave to me, and actually could not understand how the man could have been convicted by the Lord from what I said in my prayer. But God knew how to reach him. Also, we always want to pray for people, even if we don't know the details of the situation, and don't have time to ascertain them. In this case, in the space of about two minutes of prayer, God completed turned that marriage around.

Case 6: The situation

You have an impression that the Lord wants to give a word to a particular person through you. However, you don't know what the word is.

(a) What should you do?

Case 6: What happened

In a sense, this is a hypothetical case study because there are so few facts to work with. However, there was an occasion when I was in this kind of situation and the results were quite startling. But firstly, the answer to the question is that we ask the Lord what He would have us say. If He gives something to us, we can share it, but if we still have nothing we can always pray for the person. Sometimes the Lord will speak while we are praying, but even if that does not happen we can still bless the person. Praying a blessing over them is something that does not require any particular gift of the Spirit to operate and yet brings such encouragement to the person. In fact, it is a good thing to do in most ministry situations. So if you don't think the Lord has given you something, you still have a wonderful tool at your disposal. Pray God's blessing over them.

In the occasion that I referred to above, I was lying in bed and had the sense that the Lord wanted me to share something with a man I would be seeing very soon. I asked Him what I should say and the words, "Lift up your eyes," came into my mind, with the sense that God had more for him but he lacked vision and belief that God could work through him. I then asked the Lord if there was a way that I could illustrate it and He reminded me of how in my teens, I used to look at my feet when I walked. One day, I actually walked into a pole because I was not looked where I was going. That was very embarrassing, and I had long since forgotten the incident. About an hour later, my wife and I were with the man and his wife and I shared what I believed the Lord had given, and I felt somewhat foolish as I shared the illustration. He sat quietly, not really appearing to have a reaction, positive or negative, so I began to think that perhaps I had mistakenly thought the Lord had given this word to me for him. Then his wife spoke and said that she had been telling him that God had more for him and if he didn't lift up his eyes, one day he would walk into a pole. I presume that God really did have more for this man, and that he just wasn't grasping it when his wife tried to encourage him, so He gave him the same word and illustration from a different source, namely me.

eight

LEADING SOMEONE INTO
THE BAPTISM IN THE HOLY SPIRIT

I f we want to operate the gifts of the Spirit, we need to be baptized in the Spirit. This is not to limit God in what He can or cannot do, but in practice we find that we need to be baptized in the Holy Spirit in order to have a flow of the gifts in our life.

When we receive the Lord Jesus, the Holy Spirit comes into us and we are "born again," cleansed of sin, and restored to fellowship with God. In the lives of the disciples, this event took place after Jesus had risen but before He ascended to heaven. He entered the room where they were gathered and we read that "He breathed on them and said, 'Receive the Holy Spirit.'" (John 20:22). No one could be saved until Jesus had died and risen, becoming the perfect sacrifice for our sins. Therefore, although committed to the Lord, the disciples had not actually received salvation until this encounter with Him.

Subsequently, Jesus told the disciples to wait in Jerusalem until the Holy Spirit was given to them. At first, this seems like a contradiction of terms because they had received the Spirit in the room when He breathed on them, but it is not. The two events were prophesied by John the Baptist when he introduced Jesus at the beginning of His ministry. He described Jesus as "the Lamb of God who takes away the sins of the world," a reference to the Passover Lamb that typified the sacrifice made by Jesus of His own body for the forgiveness of sins. John also said that Jesus was the one who would "baptize in the Holy Spirit," referring to what would happen at the Day of Pentecost after Jesus had risen, an event that has been experienced by probably millions of Christian people since.

Jesus also used the term when instructing His disciples before His ascension. In Acts 1:5, He told them that "John truly baptized with water, but you shall be baptized with the Holy Spirit, not many days from now." John baptized people by fully immersing them in the waters of the River Jordan, and Jesus was using this water baptism as a comparison for the baptism in the Holy Spirit.

It is very clear that the apostles believed that the baptism in the Holy Spirit was an event, subsequent to being saved, and necessary in the life of believers. In Acts Chapter 9, we find Phillip in the midst of a wonderful move of God in Samaria. People were being saved, baptized in water, and delivered from demons. However, we read that none of the people had received the baptism in the Holy Spirit. Phillip and the leaders were so concerned about this that they sent for Peter and John to come and pray for the people, which they did. The people who received the baptism in the Spirit were obviously Christians because they had been baptized, yet Phillip, Peter, and John were concerned that they be baptized in the Spirit as well.

Another example is found in Acts 19:1-6. Paul met a group of people who had not been baptized in water following their becoming Christians. He counselled them, baptized them in water (so we can be sure that they were now Christians), and then prayed for them to be baptized in the Holy Spirit. Again, the baptism in the Spirit was an event, subsequent to the conversion of the people, and one that the apostle obviously deemed to be very important.

How can we lead someone into this essential experience? A simple way is to follow the words of the Lord, found in John 7:37. Jesus said, "If any man thirst, let him come to me, and drink." John immediately clarifies this by informing us that Jesus was referring to the Holy Spirit who would be given after He was glorified (in His death and resurrection).

If any man (or woman) thirst – I have met people who in so many words said that if God wanted them to be baptized in the Spirit, that was okay, but it was not something that they would actively seek. Jesus spoke of thirst, which is a very strong feeling. A person who has been without fluids for some period of time desperately wants water. Being able to quench that thirst becomes a matter of prime importance, and Jesus was telling us that being baptized in the Spirit must be something that we really want. It is not for the one with a casual approach, if it happens it happens, if it doesn't it doesn't. In fact, it behooves us to seek to be baptized in the Spirit, simply because it is a gift from God, and we should not trifle with things that He offers to us.

Let him come to Me – As John the Baptist prophesied, Jesus is the one who baptizes us in the Holy Spirit. This really makes it easy for us. We do not have to venture afar, nor do we have to perform some extreme act to show our sincerity. We simply come to Him. Isn't that what we did in order to receive salvation? It was very simple. We acknowledged our sins, asked for forgiveness, and asked Him to come into our lives. Luke wrote, "How much more will He give the Holy Spirit to those who ask Him" (Luke 11:9-13). Jesus has made it very easy for us. In fact, the simplicity of receiving the baptism in the Spirit can be a hurdle for some people because they are looking for something more complicated.

And drink – We have this desire to be baptized in the Spirit, we come to Jesus, and we ask Him to fill us. And we receive.

However, there are some occasions when people do not receive the baptism in the Spirit. There are three main reasons for this. In Acts 5:32, we read that "the Holy Spirit is given to those who obey Him," so if we are harboring some aspect of sin, refusing to give it up, we may not receive. One of the most common of these obstacles is holding a grudge against someone. We must forgive. That doesn't necessarily mean that we place ourselves in a position to be hurt over and over again, but we must forgive the person who has wronged us. God has forgiven us far more, and when teaching His disciples how to pray, Jesus said to ask for forgiveness just as we forgive others who have wronged us. The inference is that we must forgive if we want to be forgiven.

The second main reason is association with occult practices. Although all our sins are forgiven when we receive the Lord and our salvation, in practice it is common for occult practices to have to be dealt with specifically. They need to be confessed, repented of, and all contact with evil spirits renounced. Otherwise, the past involvement can be a blockage to being baptized in the Spirit.

The third main reason is preconceived notions. If we are skeptical or have some similar resistance, it is possible that we may not receive. Some people have previously been taught that the baptism in the Holy Spirit is something from the devil, a clear violation of the Bible. This can cause a person to be reticent. Part of them wants what God has for them, but part also is afraid because of what they have been taught. God is very kind, gracious, and understanding. He will help us work through these issues.

What kind of experiences do people have when they are baptized in the Holy Spirit? They vary greatly. Some people experience great joy, while the experience of others is very quiet and peaceful. Some actually have no experience at all, but soon after, they are aware of changes, such as joy, peace, the Bible becoming more real, the presence of the Lord being nearer, or a greater impact upon others when they talk about the things of God. There is no set pattern.

Is the baptism in the Holy Spirit reserved for "good" people? Not at all. As we have already observed, the apostles deemed it to be important for people to be baptized in the Spirit as soon after salvation as possible, so those people could not possibly be spiritually mature, and many of them would still have had "hangups" from their past life. We see this principle of recipients not having to be mature in their walk with God in the requirements for the Feast of Pentecost, one of three major feasts that the Israelites kept. The Holy Spirit was first given at the occasion of this feast, so it speaks to us of the baptism in the Holy Spirit. One of the requirements was that the bread that would be eaten be baked with leaven. (Leviticus 23:16-17). In the Bible, leaven is frequently a type of sin, so a person does not have to be spiritually mature to receive. They just have to be a Christian.

Another principle found in the requirements for the Feast of Pentecost is its applicability to all Christians. In

Deuteronomy 16:10-11 we find that anyone who was part of the Israelite camp could enjoy the feast. Furthermore, the apostle Peter specifically stated that the baptism in the Spirit is for all who God will call (Acts 2:38-39). So the baptism in the Spirit is for all Christians. No exceptions.

Perhaps someone understands that the apostles considered receiving the baptism in the Spirit as being important, and that it is available for all of us. But what are the benefits? We can list those that Jesus Himself described to His disciples:

- The Holy Spirit will teach them.

- He will bring things that He taught them to their remembrance.

- He will give us power. This is the power to be His witnesses, serving Him in with the demonstration of the power of God, and the power to live a holy life and become mature Christians.

We use the term, "baptism in the Holy Spirit," to describe that initial infilling as mentioned in the five instances that are recorded in the Bible and discussed below. However, looking at the benefits that Jesus listed, we see that the baptism in the Holy Spirit is very comprehensive in its application to our lives. (We should also note that while the baptism in the Spirit is the initial infilling, the book of Acts describes events where believers later received fresh infillings).

The five instances recorded in the Bible where people received the baptism in the Holy Spirit are found in the following passages:

Acts 2   The disciples on the Day of Pentecost

Acts 8   The Samaritans during the revival that was led by Phillip

Acts 9   The apostle Paul on the road to Damascus

Acts 10   The Gentiles at the house of Cornelius.

Acts 19   Certain believers in Ephesus

When we examine these events, we find certain similarities:

- The recipients were all Christians, although in the case of the Gentiles at the house of Cornelius they had probably received the Lord only minutes earlier.

- In three of the five events, they received through the laying on of hands. The two that were different really could not have involved the laying on of hands because on the Day of Pentecost, there was no one baptized in the Spirit to do so, and with Cornelius, the Holy Spirit really had to move sovereignly in order to validate that God accepted the Gentiles, just as He had accepted the Jews.

- In three of the five events, the recipients spoke in tongues. We do not know if the recipients spoke in tongues at the other two events. One of the two was Paul, and while there is no mention of tongues at the time of his being baptized in the Spirit, we know that he did receive that gift at some point (1 Corinthians 14:18). In the other event in Samaria, there is no mention of any particular gift of the Spirit, but we know something extraordinary happened because Simon the Sorcerer wanted to be able to pray for people to be baptized in the Spirit and offered money to Peter if he would give him this ability (Acts 8:18-19). Simon was so impressed by whatever happened that he wanted to have this ability and mistakenly thought he could purchase it with money.

We can also see that receiving the baptism in the Spirit was regarded as a matter of high importance by the apostles. In the case of the Samaritan Christians, the leaders of the revival were so concerned that He had not come to the new Christians that they sent to Jerusalem for Peter and John to come to help with this very issue. A similar situation occurred in Ephesus, when Paul made certain that the believers that he met not only experienced salvation but also the baptism in the Spirit. And Peter regarded the fact that the people in the house of Cornelius had been baptized in the Spirit as being a validation for them to be baptized in water to signify that they had received the Lord and their salvation.

From these five events, we can conclude that the most common way for people to receive the baptism in the Spirit is through the laying on of hands, and that the recipients will speak in tongues, at least in most instances.

I know of a number of sensible Christians who are mature in their walk, who firmly believe that they did not speak in tongues until some period of time after they had been baptized in the Spirit. I do not question their conviction. I believe that we can all speak in tongues at the time we are baptized in the Spirit, but for some reason this is not always the case. However, if we do not speak in tongues, it does present a difficulty in verifying that we have indeed been baptized in the Holy Spirit. There are other evidences, such as the presence of the Lord becoming more real, and overcoming areas of sin or weakness in our lives when before we had struggled. Speaking in tongues, however, is the clear and unmistakable evidence that a person has been baptized in the Holy Spirit.

So what is speaking in tongues? The apostle Paul referred to speaking "with the tongues of men and of angels" (1 Corinthians 13:1), so we know that this is a gift whereby we speak a language, possibly even an angelic language. The language that we speak is not one that we have learned. In is unknown to us, but may be recognized by others who hear. I know of several such instances. One of these involved a lady from a remote Middle Eastern village who heard another Christian speaking in her own dialect, telling her how to receive the Lord. In another, I personally recognized Latin as a language being spoken when someone gave a message in tongues (Latin was a compulsory subject for me in high school through my sophomore year and I recognized some of the words when the person spoke). So if we substitute the word "language" for "tongues" perhaps it is clearer. We also need to emphasize that the language spoken is not one that we know or have learned, but one that the Holy Spirit gives to us.

We should not downplay the importance of tongues. It is one of the nine gifts of the Holy Spirit, given to us for our benefit. Like the apostle Paul, we should use it often. So how can we receive it? Firstly, we must ask the Lord to baptize us in the Holy Spirit. Sometimes the language flows at that point, but sometimes we have to exercise some faith to receive it.

Let us consider the account of the disciples in Acts chapter 2. We read, "They were all filled with the Holy Spirit and began to speak with other tongues as the Spirit gave them utterance" (Acts 2:4). Who did the speaking? The disciples. Who provided the language? The Holy Spirit.

Really, what is language? It is making sounds that form words that we understand. When we speak in our native language, English for most of us, we are making sounds that form words that we understand. So when we speak in tongues, we make sounds (like the disciples, we do the speaking), and the Holy Spirit provides the language that we speak. This may sound very unspiritual, but at some point we have to start making sounds. As we do, a language comes. If we should try to create our own language it will be full of the repetition of the same consonants, but the language that the Holy Spirit gives will have variety. We will have a very wonderful gift, one that we can use to pray in situations where we don't know how to pray, one we can use to praise and worship God, and one that builds us up. Paul wrote that "he that speaks in an unknown tongue edifies himself..." (1 Corinthians 14:4), so this gift is very valuable to strengthen us within.

nine

MOVING FORWARD

I was a very young Christian when I first saw someone ministering with the gifts of the Spirit. I had gone to a home meeting and during the evening, a man stood up and asked if he could pray for some of the people in the room. As he prayed for each one, he identified something in their life that was causing a blockage to their spiritual progress, and from the reaction of those people, it was very obvious that he could not have known these things. Being very inexperienced, I assumed that God spoke to everyone like that, (and perhaps it is true that He would like to). In time, I came to realize that what I had witnessed was the operation of one of the gifts of the Spirit, in this case, the word of knowledge, and to my surprise, I realized that not everyone heard the voice of the Lord like that man.

Nevertheless, I remember being thrilled at the prospect of God speaking to me, and the thought of being able to minister like that man captured my heart. Not too long afterward, I did begin to experience the gifts of the Spirit, and this began to develop to where it was common for the Lord to give me a word for people that I prayed for. Later however, there was a period of many years when the gifts of the Spirit operated only intermittently. This was a disappointment to me, and I believe that the main reason was a lack of opportunity. I was attending a church that believed in the baptism in the Spirit and the gifts of the Spirit, but provided no environment where they could operate. It was not something that the pastor really valued, so the opportunities to pray for people were few.

Some years later still, my wife and I had moved and were now in a church that encouraged the flow of the gifts of the Spirit. Before long, I seemed to pick up the lost thread and in time, a consistency emerged, albeit a scary one because I had to actually be in the act of praying for the person before the Lord would speak to me. I became comfortable with this, and began to hear His voice more clearly, most commonly in a word of wisdom and the gift of prophecy. The same was true of my wife, through whom the Lord would speak clearly with a word of knowledge.

I have recounted this story to illustrate the importance of two things in developing our ability to minister to people. The first is actually having a desire to minister with the gifts of the Spirit. It needs to be something that we want, and as Jesus promised, we will receive if we ask, seek, and knock. The second is to be in a place where ministry is encouraged. We may even be in a church that values ministry with the gifts of the Spirit, but we still have to become involved. If we do not place ourselves in a position where we have the opportunity to minister, we will not develop. We have to become familiar with hearing the voice of the Lord, and that familiarity comes just like it does with people. We learn someone's voice by hearing it often.

Ministering to people is a privilege, and it is also a great blessing, both to them and to us. It is my sincere desire that reading this book will have encouraged you to begin your own journey to become an effective servant, equipped with the gifts of the Spirit that God has chosen to operate through you.